Sailing
for Ithaca

Sailing for Ithaca

poems by
Abayomi Animashaun

Black
Lawrence
Press

www.blacklawrence.com

Executive Editor: Diane Goettel
Book and cover design: Amy Freels
Cover art: *Placing the Moon* by Jeff Faust

Published 2014 by Black Lawrence Press.
Printed in the United States.

for
Emily

Contents

Memoir   1

In the Other Nigeria
A Way of Seeing   5
In the Other Nigeria   6
Homecoming   7
Beggar's Colony   8
Autopsy   10
4 A.M.   12

Solomon's Montessori School
The Cult of Don Quixote   17
Solomon's Montessori School   18
Honesty is the Best Policy   20
Only Humiliation   22
How We Know We Are Forgiven   25
The Measured Notion of One's Self   26

Telling Your Life Story to a Dog
In Bed with Cavafy   31
To My Friend with the Blue Hijab   33
This Woman with the Issue of Blood   35
Dining with a Stutterer   37
The Uncle   39
Telling Your Life Story to a Dog   40

And They Lived Happily Ever After

Pastime   45

National Poet   47

The Thief   49

The First Little Pig   51

And They Lived Happily Ever After   53

Sorrow   55

A Male Child of Athena

This Robe in the Temple of Apollo   59

A Descendant of Palamedes   61

Once A Year on the Island of Polyphemus   63

Taking a Siren on a Date   65

No Traveler Ever Returns Home the Same   67

A Male Child of Athena   70

Dancing to the Wrong Music

Memorizing Poems   73

Being Sure   74

Silence   76

Dancing to the Wrong Music   77

Leaving the Festival   78

Glossary   80

Acknowledgments   81

Memoir

for Chinua Achebe

Born Nigerian, my masters were confronted
With cultural subjugation and political tyranny

And thus, arrived at the fundamental credo—
Our cultures too exist.

And—
Democracy. Democracy. Democracy.

Through long sojourns within their forests and seas,
I've stumbled upon the brown scrolls of my soul,
And read their blue prophecies.

Each saying—
Seek the country within.

I'm going.

Let all who follow come as they are.
Teacher. Technician. Watchman . . .

Treat these songs as you like.
Hack them with scythes.

Loosen and say them as slang.
Whatever you like.

Enter where you can.
Leave in delight.

In the Other Nigeria

A Way of Seeing

If at night you enter a forest with a lantern—
Flame, risen and warm against the glass—

And the mast of that ship within you is blown,
Caught, and alive with wind,

Pull your oars in
From *Reason's* sea.

If later within that lantern,
The flame thins and dies,

Owls from the deck's dark corners will emerge,
Singing like your dead grandfather,

Playing flutes like his wives,
Drunk and dancing upon the stern.

In the Other Nigeria

After elections,
Instead of gathering ballots
And painting blue votes red,

Paying to blot out opponents' faces
Or marking them "X",

Politicians take balloons to each house,
Play *cops and robbers* with children,
And sing nursery rhymes.

They wink at lesbians.
Drink with homosexuals.

Hang up their coats
And join old men at farms.

They rake gutters.
Sweep yards.

Take mortars from old women
And pound yam.

They eat cold soup
With the poor in town

And leave office
With the exchequer intact.

Homecoming

It's evening. Lagos heat has cooled. At least slightly.

Mama Sule, with a wide iron ladle is turning bean cakes in hot grease.

Mama Risi is beside her talking, perhaps again of Baba Sule leaving.

They see us coming.

Mama Sule turns to Mama Risi. Her voice rises—

"Look at them. China Banana and Monkey."

"*Ssh*! They'll hear you."

"So? Let them hear me. *Chin-chin-chun* and him."

"We better smile and wave."

They look our way. Smile. Wave.

My Korean wife and I do the same.

They continue—

"Of all the girls in America, why must he marry Bruce Lee?"

"I don't know my sister. America makes them foolish."

Beggar's Colony

When it rains,
Gutters here swell
Break their ledge

And flood apartments
With feces and rodents.

The residents don't scream
Pack their clothes
And run out of buildings.

They sleep through it.
And kick gently
If the rodents get bold enough
To bite their feet.

But on such days
When the moon allows,

And is bright
Large
And free of clouds

Everyone,
Even the cripples
And the blind, crawl
And stagger outside.

The leper from *Building A*
Reaches into her blouse
Pulls a small plastic bag
With soiled cakes,

Opens it,
And shares with a blind man.

Across the street,
The cripple from *Building F*
Is laughing at an old woman

For running after a car
While holding her child
With an amputated arm.

The children,
After chasing rodents
In the water,

Take their begging bowls,
Jump in the gutters
And splash each other for hours
Till they're called back inside.

Autopsy

The students were eager
When the bearers

Laid the victim's body
On the operating table

In the left wing theatre
Of the Lagos Teaching Hospital.

Having examined hundreds like him,
The students were confident

What they'd pull and study
When they opened his spleen.

Some were even scribbling
Before his body was brought in—

The *buba* he wore
As school uniform

Mounds of *eba*
Dipped in *egusi*
He fed his dog

Flora sown
On his map
Of Lagos—

But, barely was the dermis lifted
Before reeds fell out,

Bowls from Phoenicia,
Robes from Gomorrah,

Lemons,
Guavas,

And portraits of *September*
Fanning her clit

With feathers plucked
From Gabriel's wings.

4 A.M.

Even in the other Nigeria,
Where few are bound,

And the sun,
When it desires,
Dims its own light,

Even here,
Many get up at this hour
To engage in their own ritual—

The muezzin
Calls apples to prayers,

Imams remove their beards,
Paint their faces white,

And sit in long rows
Outside mosques for hours

Till from their silences
A parade of zebras emerge.

Slowly at first,
In ones.

Then in twos,
Resolved.

Followed by mimes
Doing cartwheels,

Mangos throwing confetti,
Guavas juggling hats,

And elephants,
Pink and small as ants,

Hauling, with their trunks,
The first hours of dawn.

Solomon's Montessori School

The Cult of Don Quixote

Here, we paint our lips blue,
Our faces yellow,
Wear *silence* as garment,
And lace lemons around our necks.

And after *feeling up* pears,
We kneel by the candelabra
And pray for visions of his holiness
Sitting shirtless,

Gallant by his roiled stead,
Wearing papered armor as skirt,
Pouring wine for fat angels
He hopes to bed.

After the ritual,
We practice the stern
And furrowed expressions
Of the sane,

Open our visors, fold our lances,
Erase drawings of giants,
Bow to each other,
And walk out of the shrine.

Solomon's Montessori School

The school is popular among children.
And upon their gathering,
Each swears of her own experience—

"Yesterday, I saw ten golden gates
Standing without fences"

"Today, I saw god appoint Winds as sages"

"I've seen angels floating east"—

To suppress these claims,
Wise men from town

Stand children against the wall
Without food, for hours

Until each confesses a change of heart—
To the relief of parents
And the esteemed Council of The Wise—

That Solomon's school never existed
And is only seen by the mad.

Precisely at that moment,
A girl hears Solomon's invisible call.

She pulls down her veil,
Listens to the hymns,

Then runs like one *taken*
To begin studies

"In how to climb god's fences
And wrestle with Winds."

Honesty is the Best Policy

For years he's walked the towns,
Holy book in hand,
Speaking of the coming kingdom
And his *blessed father.*

"Afraid of the executioner?" He'd ask
"Better to tell the truth and die
Than suffer eternity under god's wrath
In lakes of burning fire."

So, I told him everything
When truth about his wife came out—

How she grabbed me from behind.
How we ran around his house,
Drank several bottles of wine,
And rode each other for hours—

I believed so fully in his mantra
And so feared god's lake of burning fire
That I showed how I pinned her to the ground
Held her breasts and towered inside her.

Telling him, I felt full contrition.
Felt purged of all demons.
Thus, I expected him to say

"I forgive as my father does.
Go. Follow his words."

But, he threw an uppercut
And broke my jaw.

Stomped on my face till I saw black
Where blue was.

I crawled out,
When he left to grab his gun.

Only Humiliation

Only humiliation will suffice
After taking your neighbor's wife,
In his house, when he's at work
In the next town on a farm.

No bushels of wheat or silver,
Prized sheep, oxen, or guinea-fowl,
Will placate his need for vengeance
Once you're found out

And are summoned by the elders
To the town square or agora,
Where the neighbor's friends,
Still hardened with rage

Are already burning effigies
Of you and the man's wife
And whacking them
With chains—

A gesture meant,
No doubt,
To pressure the elders
Into taking a tough stance

On whether you should
Be stoned with guavas,

Stripped naked and jeered,
Or flogged for hours—

Only digging your face, say,
In the feces of your neighbor's out-house
Or sitting naked for days
In his pig sty,

Might lessen his need for blood
When the final vote is cast
And you're found guilty
By the elders.

If you're lucky,
This same man
Will speak on your behalf
Saying he's dropped the charge

And remind everyone
How ashamed you are and
What you've put yourself through
In the past month and a half.

If you're lucky,
And no stone is cast,
If the elders vote to abstain
And the effigies are pulled down,

Don't even begin to think
All is forgiven

And you're now in the clear.
The day after the trial,

Return to the man's house
Before he wakes for the farm.
Wipe his windowsill and doorpost
With your sole expensive coat.

Rake dung from his yard.
Remove your blouse
And use it to wipe the walls
Of his outhouse.

How We Know We Are Forgiven

We know when our words
Are finally allowed
To travel routes of the heart
That once were barricaded
Against them as strangers
And they are given reign again
To stretch out upon sands,
Chat with newly arrived travelers,
And left alone to haggle
With silk and spice merchants.

Instead of being kicked
From tents and caravans,
Our words will once again
Be pulled into the crowds
By friends left behind,
Wiped clean of grime
Collected in the desert,
Then given fresh robes and pants,
Before being led unto hammocks to snore
After bread and wine.

The Measured Notion of One's Self

How blessed the man,
Who despite praise,
Acclaim and applause

Remains in the end,
Essentially as he was—

Unaffected by the ribbons
Taped to his door,

The bouquet of flowers,
The certificates framed
In his halls,

And in his study,
The hung medallions.

Not for this man
The relief of being paraded
Through town on borrowed horse

All for being the first of its sons
To sail the Indian Ocean *and*
The first to write several volumes
Scholars hold in high estimation.

Quite admirable that after waving
Through the confetti and horns,
He returns home not thinking
"Tomorrow praise is again assured."

But that it is already gone
And he is again as he was.

No wonder he is now at his door
Untaping the ribbons.

No doubt he's taken down
The medallions.

In the morning,
He'll return the horse.

Telling Your Life Story to a Dog

In Bed with Cavafy

After pleasing each other,
We laid in bed a long time . . .

Curtains drawn,
Bolt fastened,

We'd been cautious,
Had made a show for others—

We ordered meat and wine
From the local restaurant.

And, like other *guys*, we talked loud
About politics into the night,

But whispered about young men
We'd *bent* in the dark.

At midnight, when from the bars, drunks
Staggered onto the streets,

We shook hands the way they did,
Laughed *their* prolonged laughs,

And warned each other to steer clear
From loose girls and diseases—

All the while knowing
He'll circle round as planned,

Sit in the unused shack behind my house
Till my neighbors' candles are blown out.

And, after his soft knock,
I'll slowly release the latch
As I did last night.

To My Friend with the Blue Hijab

I love how you fall back on the bed laughing,
Press pillow against your face,
Just to break open in guffaws,
Tears streaming.

This, the third time you're telling the story—
Of the child, who, curious to learn
If veiled women have breasts,

After bets with friends,
Followed you through each stall
In the market.

But because the veil never stopped you
From being mischievous,

You turned around,
Jiggled your breasts,
And growled like a lion.

You're smiling now
As you pull the hijab
And shake loose your hair.

And I can't stop thinking of the child
Who'll return to her friends
And swear

"Muslim women are animals
Who run after children.

"They eat wood, crawl,
Jiggle their breasts,
And growl like lions."

Smiling, you toss the hijab on the couch,
Stroll into the kitchen,
And return with a single glass.

We pour wine. Cut fruit.
And talk into the night.

This Woman with the Issue of Blood

Given her country and time
She has winged maxi-pads
Pony-stamped tampons
But wouldn't mind
Nor, would I
If some messiah opened our door
Raised his hands
And said: "Do you believe child."
She, "Yes, lord."
He, "You're healed.
Go, and sin no more."
Then, Holy Midol
That disciple so terrible at its calling
Would shrivel in the prison walls
Of the cupboard and collect dust.
Not to mention St. Tylenol
Whom we'd manacle, blindfold
March to the edge, then kick
Into the water-filled funnel.
Then *she*—you
Wouldn't feel *an urge,* this month
To knife my suit.
All for a milk grime
Spilled yesterday
In one of your shoes.
You'll hold me instead

Against your chest
To trace the length
And kiss the tiny boulders
Of your small breasts.

Dining with a Stutterer

I too am one
And would love you to think

Since I *tense*
Then stump my feet for speech

god chose poor clay
To mold me,

My mother smoked
When I was conceived,

I fail
At *normal thinking*,

And can't help grabbing my crutch
And saying "s-s-screw this"

Or about your dress,
"i-i-it's damn ugly."

Don't buy it.

Interrupt me as you would
Any other person.

Mock my corny jokes
And flat punch lines.

When I say
"f-f-fuck you,"

Comeback with a
"Fuck you too."

And for good measure,
"Stupid bastard."

And if I ignore all you're saying,
Yet remark
"y-you have gr-great tits."

Slap me the way you would
Any other person.

Dump wine on my head.
Pasta on my shirt.

Make your message clear.

Or I'll keep trying,
Hoping to get away with worse,

Thinking you a fool,
Until you catch on.

The Uncle

He is well in his sixties
And walks around town
With the same scholar's acumen
As when he was thirty.

From a basket
He's woven a crown.

And flies buzz in salute
When he wades into gutters
For feces at night.

Last seen, he foamed
Froth at the mouth,
Was wearing mud as eyeliner,
And was chasing girls from farms . . .

And what coincidence!
Here he comes.

Naked as the day he was born,
Chewing stick
Like it's roasted corn,

Waving his baton
Ahead of a procession
Of dead choir boys.

Telling Your Life Story to a Dog

You begin with that moment in grade school
When, sitting in the middle row
You dropped your lunch money by the popular girl's desk
And bent, for that glorious chance to glimpse
Her pink polka-dotted underwear.

You don't leave out that afternoon when
Food fight turned sour and the pupils in class
After being asked how it began
Broke from silence, pointed at you
And said "he was the first to spray water and throw rice."

And you continue about how
Instead of writing three-syllable words in class.
You drew stick figures of you and your big breasted teacher
Wearing ski masks, breaking into banks,
And making away with quinzillion dollars.

You go on and on about
Barely being able to read
And how little you cared back then
For books on science experiments
And the stupid practice called "hygiene."

Only hours later, do you realize
Your old friend—

The dog,
Much unconcerned with your story,
But too polite to leave—

Is resigned beside you asleep.
His food bowl empty.
His flavored bone chewed thin.

And They Lived Happily Ever After

Pastime

After rolling our *joys* in mud,
We dry them for a few hours.

Sure the consistencies have taken,
Each does with his as he pleases.

Oil palm traders use theirs
To crack open kernels.

Some toy makers glue on
Tiny shoes and pants,

While others fit them
With small pink hats.

Children from different yards
Play a complex game of catch,

Five or more to a team,
With marked boundary lines.

The prince paints his the city flag
And rolls it on the ground

When tributes come in
From military pacts.

The king uses his,
As best he can, for pillow

When he's asleep
And drooling on the throne.

National Poet

Gone are the days
When his work was read
By the President

Who made a habit
Of giving him medals
For unwritten poems

Gone the flutists
Playing his verse

The banquets endorsed
By congress.

These days he
Walks around town

And is hailed
By young writers
Eager for autographs

And well-wishers
Waving flags.

In the evenings
He returns home

And after dinner
Sets about some verse

He hopes will win praise
Like those from years past.

After hours staring
At the same lines

His neck slouches
His eyes give

And he starts snoring
On the couch dreaming—

This time, he's inside
The Presidential Villa

With emissaries
From neighboring towns

Nodding to his famous poems,
Set to music and played
By ferrets and field mice.

The Thief

He is a good man, with only one wife
And two boys and one girl from her.
Unlike his peers who stay out till dark,
Drinking and shooting dice at the local bar,
He's always home by five
In time to join his family for supper
And, hours later, to follow his young son,
Training to be a rabbi,
To the synagogue in the next town.
You can usually hear him miles from his house
Uttering strange noises
While praying to god, his *heavenly father.*
No other man is the envy of all wives
Than this man, who on Sundays
Can be seen in the yard
Sorting laundry with his wife.
No other parent is more sought after
At the children's schools for functions,
Contributions, and dinners.
Not to mention the art he's donated
To the local museum, or the cars
He's given to the crippled and blind.
Even on days he resumes his trade
And must travel to the next town
To hijack traders, he is kind about it.
Gentle. So soft spoken that
If not for the machete in his hand

His prey would see him no doubt
As *another* fallen victim to highway robbers.
But, he's finished this morning
And is back home already.
His blade rinsed and wiped clean,
He is busy in the kitchen
Making eggs for his wife, still asleep,
Who will soon wake up demanding coffee.

The First Little Pig

Let's reenter the story,
Knowing

The spirit that led him to straws
Led the other to bricks.

That his quiet steady fitting of each bundle
Came from within.

How stubborn he must have been
Knowing in what degrees,

When summoned by the Wolf,
The wind thickens.

How foolish,
Yet courageous,

For him to sit
In his own frail construction

While the Wolf playfully taps
On his straw walls,

Summons all breath,
And blows down his door

Just to turn around
And lift him off the floor

Wipe dirt from his face
Rinse from his hands
Bruises and scrapes

Before fanning coals
In the hearth for flame,

Where this little pig knows
He'll be boiled

As the Wolf contemplates
Which of his ears
He'll tear off first.

And They Lived Happily Ever After

Doesn't mean they are
In the room right now

Naked, *Wrestling*,
Saying,

"You like that?"
"Yeah."

"Go slower?"
"Pound it."

Or that his gaze at this maid's
Pointed breasts
Or that one's,
So full against her cheap dress

Is a mistake,
A chance occurrence.

But that, just three years
after going door to door
With the glass slipper

Testing each maiden's foot
To find his *mystery* woman

He's the one fat
From inactivity. Boring

From the same speech.
Remarkably dull in his musings . . .

And she, once he starts snoring
Will again slip through doors

Past corridors
Into a room with another male servant
Where, unlike the ones from nights previous,

She hopes to be thrown to the floor
The royal bra ripped from her chest
Her legs spread and hemmed against the wall.

Sorrow

Try this—

Instead of locking *it*
In the basement of your house,

Give *it* the same uniform
You wore as a child.

The same coat, socks,
And school bag.

Difficult as it must be
And may sound,

Send *it* out of the house

With the simple truth
That, like *it*,

There are others
At this hour

Going to the same school,
Up the block,

A mile down.

Don't rush *it* out, or coax
In a voice too loud.

When *it's* ready,
Watch

As *it'll* break off fear
And join the crowd

Shake hands with others
And strike up friendships

Right there
Outside your house

Laughing
To jokes told

In the warm
Morning light.

A Male Child of Athena

This Robe in the Temple of Apollo

Must be picked up gently
And worn with care

Not soaked in bleach
Painted in bright colors
And displayed at the square

Beside silks
Precious stones
And gold belts.

Pulled slowly from the rack
Taken across each arm
And worn as is

Seeds within you
Will roll on soil,
Sink,

And break into trees,
With leaves composed
Of all before
And never has been,

High and large enough
For you and your unborn twin
To sit and argue beneath,

Chase each other around,
Pull each branch and climb,
In games of *hide and seek*.

A Descendant of Palamedes

How disappointing it must be
To learn you're a descendant
Of Palamedes,

After years of combing archives
And mapping each branch
Of your family tree,

Examining each leaf
And tracing your lineage
Across the Atlantic
To Bronze Age Greece—

With its stock of heroes
Whose failures and deeds
We continue to read
And marvel at still

Priam, Hector,
Briseis,
Ajax, Nestor,
Achilles.

How disappointing
That of all these
You're a descendant
Of Palamedes—

The also-ran
Responsible for calling out
The king of Ithaca

In his two-paragraph cameo
In Apollodorus' *Bibliotheca*.

An ancestor, if we are to surmise,
Capable of peering through
The most planned out guile
But lacking foresight

To stay silent on what he finds
Forgetting not all truths
Must be shared or spoken alike.

What reputation to have.
And it's no wonder, good friend,
You've become iron-clad—

Silent on why
I turned up shirtless
This morning outside my house
After spending all night at the bar.

What welcome change you are
To that progenitor of your line,

Who would have told my wife
I wasn't attacked by robbers
But bartered my shirt for wine.

Once a Year on the Island of Polyphemus

Once a year on the Island of Polyphemus,
Tourists make the long trek to the cave
Where the Cyclops imprisoned Odysseus
And tore and bit into the hero's sailors
After bashing their skulls to pulp.

They take pictures of giant boulders,
Cauldrons, prisoner markings
Upon cave walls, and dugout fossils
Experts claim are remnants of loin cloths.

Always, around midnight, the guide
Falls asleep from too much wine.
Then others, just as drunk, jump ship
And trek back to the cavern,

Where the men have pissing contests
By the entrance. Not to be outdone,
The women remove their bras
And take turns crawling "like sheep"
Around each boulder.

Again this year,
The ship sails without them.
The guide wakes from his stupor,
Washes his face, and walks to deck.

He looks through the telescope—

Near shore, he sees the Cyclops
Swimming near sea gulls. Higher up,
He sees "the chosen ones"
Still naked, asleep, and drunk.

The guide shrugs, closes the telescope,
And staggers into the lounge.
He orders omelet, water, and more wine,
Sits, away from the television, in the corner,

Opens his *Handbook for Tour Guides*,
And pencils a few notes in the marginalia,
About Odysseus's sailors and a school of swine,
As the ship continues past mid-sea
Toward Circe's Island.

Taking a Siren on a Date

You need not plug your ears with wool
Or bind your chest to a chair's rest
From fear, when she starts talking,

Of plunging into your bowl of soup,
Ramming your head against the table
And splintering your skull with wood.

When she comes in, speak to her
In a manner so reckless and sure
She knows from the outset
You're no Odysseus.

Make clear that as god is your witness
You'll leap into the waters first
Before you lose your right mind
To her songs or laments.

Hell, show her your mind
Wasn't right to begin with
By talking of rivers in your town
That lean on trellises,

How you comb sea-horses
On your chin each morning,
And of blue vines and clay buttons
Boats wear when professing love
To lemons, pears, and donkeys.

And if she is incapable of realizing
You're too far gone to be threatened
By her singing,

Stand her up. Leave.
Don't worry about her weeping alone
By her free drink. Soon,

She'll find one like the son of Laertes—
Who conquered the Aegean
But never found the Ithaca within.

No Traveler Ever Returns Home the Same

He arrives
With a different Light

Dimmer in kind
Than the one he had

When the ship took wind
And he waved a last time

To his loved ones
And folks from town

Standing on the harbor,
Blended with the night,

Hoarse from "farewell"
And "god speed"

Shivering in thin coats
Till the boat leaves.

That young man,
Like this one—

Wearing polished boots
And blue earrings,

Lying in drunken stupor
Near a flute beside me—

Will carry with him
Memories from the sea

And days on land,
In cities,

Where he gambled
His meager wages.

Gone forever is the child
Whose flute,

In the synagogue,
Accompanied words

The elders wrote
And taught.

Even when his loved ones
And town folks gather—

As they surely must
When he arrives—

And ask for one song
He played as a child

That song will carry
Days he slept alone in bars,

Mornings he woke up
In a hooker's lace bra,

Nights on cannabis alone
After dancing naked

Round burn-fires
With a beauty called Calypso,

And those evenings
Without wine

When he'd kiss
And love a man

And pretend
It's the first time.

A Male Child of Athena

No matter his constitution,
Whether returning from Troy

Or drunk again and chasing
Naked women outside a pub,

After finally arriving
And finding peace on his shores—

Kissing his old wife
And embracing a Telemachus—

He too must offer barley,
White cloth,

Fattened calf,
And barrels of oil

Raised on a pyre and burned
To appease his Poseidon.

Dancing to the Wrong Music

Memorizing Poems

It is no different than lighting a candle
And holding it high to see better
The inner doorway of the heart—

Its red knob. Framed trellis.
The names of ancestors penciled
In yellow and purple calligraphy.

Holding that lit candle
The door melts,
And you find yourself
In the market of an ancient city

Teeming with people of all ethnicity
Peddling tomatoes. Onions. Silks.
Sandals. Drums. Saffron. Milk . . .

You walk around for hours.
Tired, you sit on a bench.
Then notice, in an empty stall
Away from the noise,

A girl wearing braids
Playing with her veil
The way your mother did
When about her age.

Being Sure

At its whitest, searing,
And most hot

It is a clear signal of one
Lacking the wisdom

To rest in silence
And look on

When friends fail
And return home distraught

Telling,
Without being asked,
All they've done

Speaking quietly
Like those in church
Inside a contraption

Separating priest
From confessor.

No different from when
Your neighbor

Talked with straight face
About loving a child

Or the ex-Mayor
Owning up

To multiple
Teenage wives.

Not now
Cutting with

"Why do this"
"You should know better"

"Recite Hail Marys and
Our fathers."

Not this
To ones who,
In a sense,

Rowed rivers
To find you

Known to stay silent
And listen

Who, himself,
Doesn't have much clue

And must sail
His own seas.

Silence

When learning is surrendered
At your gates

And one stays for months
Years and days

You become the destination
And the halfway point.

The lamp
The over-grown path

The pond
And the clear night-sky.

You become the open field
The thick brush

The village
Where nothing lives

The wilderness
Where all is born.

Dancing to the Wrong Music

It's the same as tying fish
Around your waist
And running a gentle race.

Mastered,
From your chest
Waters roil awake

And become streams
That circle old trees
Till their leaves turn green.

Leaving the Festival

Farewell to the masquerades,
Their sequined costumes,
Their guttural-voiced songs
That frighten and delight people.

So long to the acrobats and their flips.
The fruit jugglers and their game
Of tossing orange. Guava. Peach.

Time for magicians who soared
And disappeared among clouds,
To return from the heavens
And remove their moustache.

Time for young men and women
To roll and stack mats,
Arrange chairs in a corner,
And rake filth from grass.

For those too drunk
To make the long trek back,
Time to wipe drool
From their hands,
And cover their heads with hats. Time

For children to return frocks
To Spanish squires,

For Christians to reclaim their stern brows
And give naked Arabs their turbans.

Time for each to leave the grounds,
Walk with friends as far as he can,
Before taking the lonely road
Back to his own town.

Glossary

Homecoming

Mama Sule—Sule's Mother

Baba Sule—Sule's Father

Mama Risi—Risi's Mother

Chin-chin-chun—A derogatory imitation of the Chinese language

Autopsy

Buba—A loose blouse or garment worn by adults and children

Eba—A dish made from cassava flour or *garri*

Egusi—A type of soup made with melon or pumpkin seeds

Acknowledgments

Many thanks to the journals, where these poems first appeared in their early or final forms:

A Way of Seeing: *Passages North*. The Thief: *5 A.M*. Memoir: *The James Dickey Review*. Beggar's Colony: *The Cortland Review*. The Cult of Don Quixote: *Cerise Press*. Memorizing Poems. This Woman with the Issue of Blood. Telling Your Life Story to a Dog. And They Lived Happily Ever After: *Diode*. How We Know We Are Forgiven. The Measured Notion of One's Self: *Jaded Ibis*. To My Friend with the Blue Hijab. In Bed with Cavafy. Solomon's Montessori School. Honesty is the Best Policy. The First Little Pig: *The Adirondack Review*. National Poet. A Descendant of Palamedes. *Mount Hope*. Dancing to the Wrong Music: *North Dakota Quarterly*.

Special thanks also to David Shumate and Allison Wilkins. Joseph Harrington and Byron Caminero-Santangelo. Alex Gubbins and Folabo Ajayi. Colin Christopher and Jeremy Miller. "Buzz" Minnick and Alice Shelton. Shelley Puhak and Beverly Matherne. Black Lawrence Press. Angela Leroux-Lindsey and Diane Goettel.

To my father, Mukaram, *iyin at'ope*
To my dear siblings, Seun and Sanmi, *eyin lashoo mi*
To my mother, Arike, *oosha biiya 'osi*

Abayomi Animashaun is also the author of *The Giving of Pears*. A winner of the Hudson Prize and a recipient of a grant from the International Center for Writing and Translation, Animashaun teaches at the University of Wisconsin, Oshkosh and lives in Green Bay, Wisconsin.